MEET
JOHN
CENA

S0-BKI-008

SCHOLASTIC INC.

ISBN 978-1-338-66791-2

10 9 8 7 6 5 4 3 2 1   20 21 22 23 24

Printed in the U.S.A.   40
First printing 2020

Book design by Fabia Wargin Design
Written by Devra Speregen

Everything about John Cena is BIG.

His muscles are BIG.

His performance in the ring is BIG. His presence in movies and TV shows is BIG.

But what people are always surprised to learn about this famous wrestler, author, rapper, and film and TV star is that the biggest thing about him is . . . his heart!

John Cena has spent over seventeen years as a professional wrestler with World Wrestling Entertainment (WWE), where he is mostly known for his tough-guy image and being tied as the most decorated wrestler of all time.

In movies and on television he often plays big, brawny, and comedic no-nonsense characters, too. But the image John has in the ring and onscreen couldn't be further from who he really is. Behind John's tough exterior is a thoughtful, caring, and generous guy!

"Never forget you have value," is one of the messages Cena regularly tweets. "Be brave enough to admit and face failure, and it may just reward you with the wisdom to achieve your dreams." John's days are filled with charitable work for many different and deserving groups, such as organizations that support terminally ill children and the armed services.

So, how did this "tough guy" with huge muscles and an intimidating persona morph into one of today's kindest, most beloved celebrities?

Take a behind-the-scenes look at the many faces of John Cena and see for yourself. Behind the gruff pro-wrestling superstar-turned-movie-star persona, John Cena has been a super sweet softie the whole time!

PROFILE

Name: John Felix Anthony Cena Jr.

Weight: 251 pounds

Birthdate: April 23, 1977

Current Home: Tampa, Florida

Birthplace: West Newbury, Massachusetts

Height: 6 feet, 1 inch

Family: (parents) Carol and John Felix Anthony
(siblings) Stephen, Dan, Matt, and Sean

Hobbies: Collecting muscle cars, learning Mandarin, and playing the piano

Earliest jobs: Fitness attendant at Gold's Gym, limousine driver

Favorite Teams: Boston Bruins, Boston Red Sox, Tampa Bay Rays, Los Angeles Dodgers, New England Patriots, and Boston Celtics

Moment He'll Never Forget: When he got the chance to throw the first pitch out for the Los Angeles Dodgers in 2009, and he threw it to his childhood hero and former first baseman Don Mattingly

Did You Know? He writes with his left hand, throws with his right, and favors his right arm when wrestling.

Favorite Ice Cream: Ben & Jerry's Chunky Monkey

Funny Celebrity Endorsement: In 2016, Cena was the voice of Ernie the Elephant in a TV commercial campaign for Wonderful Pistachios®.

THE NICEST TOUGH GUY IN THE RING!

As a wrestler, Cena became known for inventing Reverse Trash Talk! John explained the skill on a talk show. John says it's when you're in someone's face like a mad, intimidating wrestler, but instead of saying mean things in your loud, angry voice, you say *nice* things! He gave an example of how he's mastered this technique by doing a Reverse Trash Talk to an audience member. First, he stared the guy down; then he snarled and pointed his finger at him menacingly.

"Like YOU!" he growled. "Sitting there in the FIRST ROW, with your legs CROSSED and your VEST ON! You look FOCUSED! Like you're REALLY paying attention to what I'm saying! And it's making me feel GREAT!"

"And YOU!" he said, turning to the host. "Sitting there in your SUIT and your FASHIONABLE TIE! If you even look at me the way that you are, I will SMILE FROM EAR TO EAR for the rest of the evening!"

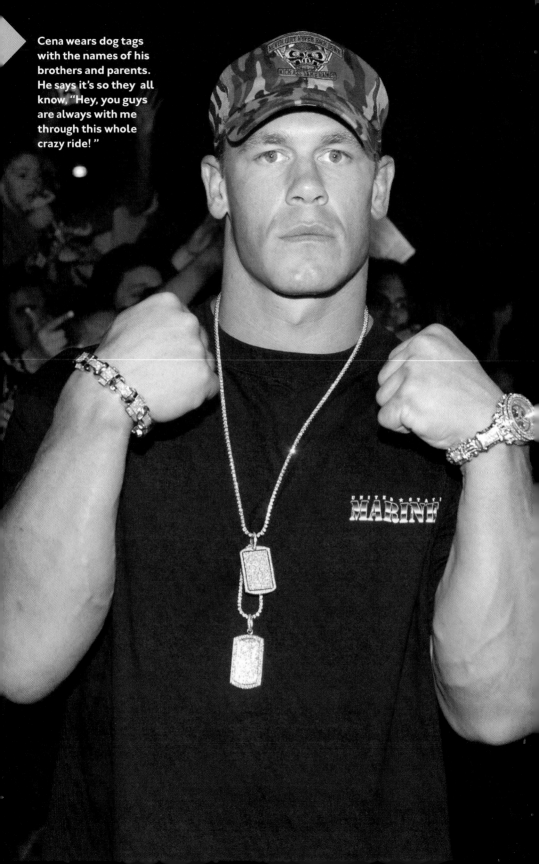

Cena wears dog tags with the names of his brothers and parents. He says it's so they all know, "Hey, you guys are always with me through this whole crazy ride!"

Roddy Piper battles Mr. T at the first Wrestlemania in 1985.

AMERICAN-MADE
MUSCLE

John Felix Anthony Cena Jr. was born in West Newbury, Massachusetts, on April 23, 1977. He was one of five boys in a competitive family. Growing up in the Cena house meant *everything* was a competition, even dinner! When food came to the table, Cena remembers, it was every kid for himself!

It was a loving home, Cena says, though living in a house with five roughhousing boys also meant a lot of fighting, bickering, teasing ... and wrestling! Like other kids, Cena and his brothers shared a love for Saturday morning cartoons, Nintendo video games like *Donkey Kong* and *Super Mario Bros.*, and baseball cards. But their greatest love was watching WrestleMania and emulating their favorite World Wrestling Foundation (WWF) superstars. *Saturday Night's Main Event*, among other TV programs, always brought the Cena boys together to watch the matches and copy their favorite wrestlers' signature moves on each other.

It might be surprising to learn that John was picked on and bullied at school as a kid.

After losing one particular fight when he was twelve, Cena remembers, he'd had *enough* and decided it was time to make a change. He idolized many of the top wrestlers on TV and knew they worked hard for their muscles. He begged his father to buy him a weight bench and a set of weights, and he started working out. Slowly but surely, Cena began to grow and sculpt his body. He recalls the moment he stepped into his high school gym and first realized he was bigger and stronger than everybody else. Nobody was messing with him or bullying him anymore.

"I know what it feels like to be knocked down," Cena tells kids today who write to him asking for advice about dealing with bullies. "But I also know what it feels like to get back up."

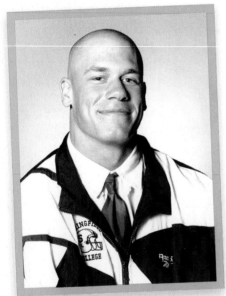

John Cena played football in high school at Cushing Academy, a private prep school in Ashburnham, Massachusetts. He went on to Springfield College in Springfield, Massachusetts, where he was an All-American offensive lineman wearing number 54.

In 1998, he graduated with a degree in exercise physiology, the study of how the body responds to physical activity. People with an exercise physiology degree can have a career in many fields, including athletic training or physical therapy, or, as in John's case, wrestling, acting, and more!

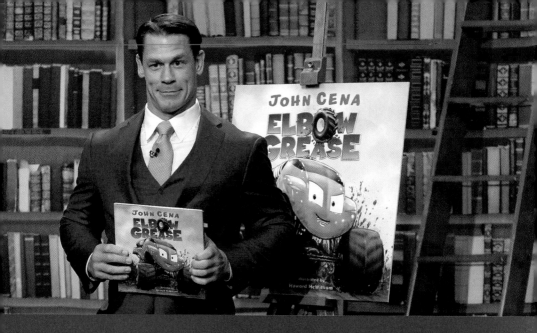

ELBOW GREASE

In addition to being a wrestler and actor, John Cena is also the author of a children's book series called *Elbow Grease*. First published in 2018, the series features a character named Elbow Grease, a brave little monster truck with four bigger brothers who is based on Cena growing up in a family with five brothers. "I'm stealing a page from my childhood and my adult life when I emphasize the importance of believing in yourself, teamwork, and never giving up," Cena says about the books.

From the get-go, he set out to write something for his youngest fans—a story that would highlight the qualities and values he stands for in a bright, colorful, and funny way.

"[The books are] about the values that it's taken me four decades on this planet to learn," Cena said in an interview. "Like, don't be afraid to try something new, because if you don't try anything new, you'll never learn anything. Don't be afraid to go out of your comfort zone." Cena hopes children who read his books will learn not to listen when others say they aren't good enough—or big enough—to do something.

"I chose a family of monster trucks because I grew up with four brothers and we each have our own distinct personality. One is super fast, one is super loud, one is super crazy." Cena gave each monster truck a personality modeled after himself and one of his brothers. There's Elbow Grease, Flash, Pinball, Tank, and Crash.

"Which truck are you?" a reporter asked him.

"Oh, Elbow Grease," Cena replied. "One hundred percent!"

THE MOVE TO
MUSCLE BEACH

After graduating from college,

Cena wrestled with a big decision: what to do with the rest of his life. He had no clue. By then he had become an accomplished bodybuilder and decided to move across the country to the center of the bodybuilding universe: Venice Beach, California—also called "Muscle Beach" because of all the bodybuilders who gather on the beach to lift weights.

Unfortunately, Cena's dad was against the idea from the start. "Sure, go on out there," his father told him. "You won't last two weeks!"

But Cena knew in his brave little monster-truck heart that his father was wrong. He believed that he was determined and disciplined enough to persevere. With just $500 in his pocket, he left Massachusetts to start a new life on the West Coast.

It wasn't an easy adjustment, but Cena made it work. He got a job folding towels and scrubbing toilets at Gold's Gym (a famous Venice Beach gym), and he worked as many shifts as he could so he could achieve his most immediate goal: moving out of his car! That's right, John Cena used to live in his 1991 Lincoln Continental. He couldn't

afford an apartment when he first moved to California, so he used the gym to shower and change and slept in his car in the parking lot.

Cena didn't mind making a few sacrifices. He loved his job at the gym and he knew his hard work would eventually pay off. In 1999, Cena had his first taste of acting when he was cast in a funny TV commercial for the gym where he worked. In the commercial, Cena oils his muscles and flexes in front of the mirrors in the gym's posing room. Then, when he confidently steps out of the room and into the gym . . . he slips and falls right in front of two women on exercise bikes!

Around the same time, one of Cena's friends mentioned a nearby wrestling training academy that taught the "secrets" of successful wrestling.

"It got to the point where I really needed to make a career out of my life," Cena recalled. "I was twenty-two years old and I needed some direction." He had considered joining the Marines. In fact, he learned about the wrestling academy on the same weekend he had been planning to enlist!

Cena and his friends always talked about the WWE, so it wasn't a surprise when one friend approached him and said, "'You look big, you talk like you know what's going on, did you ever want to try to do this?' I figured, yeah, I'll give it a shot. As soon as I saw a ring, one that I could physically get in and mess around with, I knew there was no turning back at that point!"

Cena was a natural in the ring. "I was sought out by WWE recruiters," he said. "Someone [saw me and] said, 'Hey, would you like a chance at wrestling in front of larger crowds?'"

Well . . . *DUH!*

In 2001 Cena signed with the WWF (now the WWE), and was assigned to its training facility in Louisville, Kentucky, called Ohio Valley Wrestling (OVW). He has been making a steady climb to the top of the sport ever since. He's currently one of the most recognizable pro wrestlers in the world, and in 2018 he was ranked as the highest-paid wrestler in the WWE, earning upward of $10 million a year!

DID YOU KNOW THAT JOHN CENA IS A PIZZA-EATING CHAMPION?

Zeppy's, a pizza place near John's home in Venice Beach, had a promotion: If you ate a whole pizza pie, you'd get the pizza for free. Cena says he used to go in and devour an entire pie in twenty minutes! "The [pizza parlor] guy's face dropped," Cena recalled. "He didn't realize that I was broke and hungry, so I went back the next day and did the same thing." Eventually the owner figured out that Cena didn't have the money to pay for the pizza. Luckily, he was a pretty understanding guy. He told Cena he didn't need to eat a whole pie anymore. He told Cena, "Just stop by for a free slice any time you want."

CENA'S DEBUT: "THE PROTOTYPE"

Building on an already impressively sculpted physique, bodybuilder John Cena developed his first wrestling gimmick (a wrestler's image or "act"): The Prototype. With semi-robotic movements and tons of in-your-face taunts, "The Prototype" won the Ultimate Pro Wrestling (UPW) Heavyweight Championship in 2000.

While John Cena as The Prototype may have *looked* intimidating, he could never quite stay in character as a mean, lean wrestling machine. John's genuine goofiness and funny personality always managed to shine through.

John Cena made his television wrestling debut in 2002, when Vince McMahon (left, the chairman of the WWE) agreed to let him replace a wrestler who had come down with the flu.

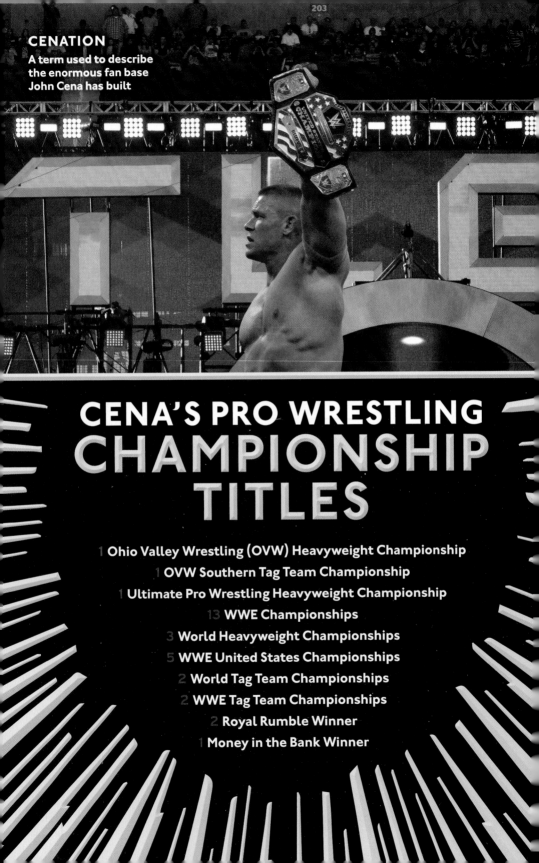

203

CENATION
A term used to describe the enormous fan base John Cena has built

CENA'S PRO WRESTLING
CHAMPIONSHIP
TITLES

1 Ohio Valley Wrestling (OVW) Heavyweight Championship
1 OVW Southern Tag Team Championship
1 Ultimate Pro Wrestling Heavyweight Championship
13 WWE Championships
3 World Heavyweight Championships
5 WWE United States Championships
2 World Tag Team Championships
2 WWE Tag Team Championships
2 Royal Rumble Winner
1 Money in the Bank Winner

CENA'S DAILY ROUTINE

What's a typical day like for John Cena?

6–7 a.m. Wake, shower, and shave.

8 a.m. Check messages and email, eat breakfast (usually a protein shake or a four-egg omelet with a sautéed vegetable), get dressed (either a suit or the "classic John Cena": T-shirt, baseball cap, and jean shorts—or, as he calls them, jorts), review schedule for the day, meditate.

9 a.m. Work out in the gym for two hours (two days per week of lower/full body, two days per week of upper/full body). If preparing for a movie, study lines.

11 a.m. Shower #2, head to business for the day (either by scheduled limo, a tour bus, or his Jeep Wrangler)

12 noon. Meal #2 (small, 230 calories, could be a protein bar or a protein shake). Run errands and touch base with family by phone.

4 p.m. Meal #3 (small, 230 calories, could be a protein bar or a protein shake).

5–7 p.m. Home, to officially end the day. Catch up with friends, practice Mandarin or piano.

7 p.m. Meal #4 (dinner, usually chicken or fish and a whole-grain side like brown rice.)

11 p.m. Bedtime.

Though he's known for his super strict diet and healthy lifestyle, not everything John Cena eats is good for him. Recently, he confessed to eating a ridiculous amount of Tic Tacs before every match! Cena says he will start eating them about three hours before a match, and typically consume about *five packs* of the mints in total!

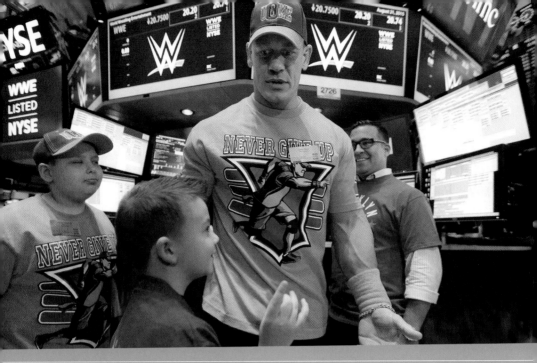

THEIR WISH
IS HIS COMMAND

The title that John Cena is most proud of is one he earned outside of the ring. Since 2004, John has worked closely with the Make-A-Wish Foundation of America® and has granted over six hundred wishes with the organization, earning him the title of Most Wishes Granted by a Celebrity!

At first John had hoped to keep these visits quiet so people wouldn't think he was just seeking publicity. But when the Make-A-Wish Foundation explained that making the visits public might encourage more donations and fund more wishes, he agreed to become a sort of ambassador for the organization.

John recognizes these kids are battling life-threatening conditions, and he knows how serious the topic is. But he focuses on what he's being asked to do—provide them with a much-needed escape—rather than dwell on the challenges of their situations. He calls the experience "magical" for the child—and for himself. "I'll do [it] for as long as I can, as long as they're asking me to," he says.

RINGSIDE WISHES

John Cena strives to make every single wish something truly special. If he's wrestling, he'll wear gifts from the Make-A-Wish kids into the ring or give them a shout-out from the mic. In 2017, he celebrated his WWE Championship win by leaping out of the ring and draping his title belt over one little boy's shoulder!

A memorable wish was when John Cena enjoyed a tea party with a seven-year-old girl. She brought a toy tea set to the meeting and Cena asked if she wanted to have a tea party. The girl's father remembers how wonderful it was to watch "a big wrestler" in full wrestling gear and knee pads sipping tea with his daughter. "Her eyes lit up like the galaxy," the girl's father said. "They were talking like they had been friends forever." He added that it's something his daughter will remember "for the rest of her life."

THE MAKE-A-WISH FOUNDATION

The Make-A-Wish Foundation is an organization that grants wishes for critically ill children. If kids want to meet their favorite athlete or celebrity, have lunch with an actor, or even take a trip to Disney World, the people who work at the Make-A-Wish Foundation try to make it happen!

CENATION-SPEAK: WORDS TO LIVE BY

From the moment he captured his first WWE Championship title, kids have idolized and adored John Cena, attending live wrestling matches in droves and showing him lots of pop! ("Pop" is a pro wrestling term for the love and admiration the crowd shows a wrestler.) It's the reason he prefers to make family-friendly films, host kids' TV shows, write children's books, and make goofy videos on YouTube that his young fans adore.

YOU CAN'T SEE ME

For more than a decade, Cenation has known the drill when John Cena heads toward the ring: You wave your hand in front of your face and you scream at the top of your lungs, "YOU CAN'T SEE ME!"

The funny thing is, while everyone knows it's Cena's most identifiable catchphrase and hand gesture, not many fans know *why*. Only recently did John spill the secret as to the origin of "You Can't See Me," admitting that it was actually part of a joke with his younger brother Sean.

In 2005, the Cena brothers were goofing around while testing out hip-hop beats for a new rap album John was recording called *You Can't See Me*. Sean started dancing around while moving his hands around his head—the way he'd seen rappers do. The brothers all laughed, and suddenly there was a dare on the table: Sean dared John to do the silly move on TV the next time he was in a WWE match.

Not one to back away from a dare, John accepted. He modified the move a bit, and like that, an iconic hand gesture was born! He did the move more and more in the ring, and pretty soon it had morphed into a Cenation rallying cry. Whenever the wrestler threw open his hand toward the arena roof, fans would shout at the top of their lungs, "YOU CAN'T SEE ME!"

"And now, for fifteen years, because of a dare, I've been doing this," John joked, waving his hand back and forth in front of his face.

WHY HE LIKES KID FANS BEST:

"I love energy and I love excitement, and I think kids have the same. They have such a lust for life, such an honest and genuine attack on every day," Cena says. "They don't hide how they feel. You can tell when a child is embarrassed. You can tell when they're excited. You can tell when they're happy, and you can tell when something you do makes them happy."

Cena says what connects him to kids most is that they're not trying to "shade you" with anything. "They'll give it to you straight. I love that honesty."

JOHN CENA
T-SHIRT MASH-UP

In 2009, after popularizing his original gimmicks in the ring, John Cena decided it was time for a change. He wanted to reveal to the world and his fans what was in his heart and help them understand his values.

John had always worn simple T-shirts with tough-guy sayings and logos during his wrestling matches. Suddenly he began wearing shirts with slogans including "Never Give Up!" and "Rise Above Hate." Bright, bold colors were always used for emphasis. Sometimes he would pair his message with a cause, like he did with "Rise Above Cancer" in 2012.

Cena wore a black-and-pink Rise Above Cancer T-shirt for a wrestling match, then donated the proceeds from every shirt sold ($1 million!) to Susan G. Komen to support breast cancer awareness.

The colorful T-shirts with a message resonated with fans immediately. A new level of excitement accompanied Cena's matches as the crowd waited for him to reveal his newest slogan along with his newest moves in the ring.

CENA STYLE

John is famous for tearing off his T-shirt and tossing it, along with his hat, into the audience as he walks toward the ring. That leaves him wearing only a few wristbands and his style signature . . . jorts! John Cena loves to wear jean shorts in the ring, and he isn't apologizing for it!

JOHN CENA VS. THE ROCK

Another popular wrestler-turned-actor

is Dwayne "The Rock" Johnson. When you compare Johnson and Cena, upon first glance they seem to be extremely similar. Many WWE fans even considered John Cena to be a Rock wannabe, since Johnson is five years older and began his wrestling and movie career many years before Cena.

"To say that I want to emulate the career of Dwayne Johnson is true in some aspects," Cena said in a 2004 TV interview. Johnson was the first wrestler brave enough to take a break from pro wrestling to try his hand at acting. Cena says that his former WWE rival is now his inspiration!

"But I also know that if you are a copy of someone, that is all you'll ever be," he added thoughtfully. "And now they are wondering who will be the next John Cena. I'm not going to be the next anybody. I'm going to be the first me!"

THE ROCK-CENA RIVALRY

The rivalry between John Cena and The Rock began in 2008, when Cena made it clear in an interview that, although he admired The Rock's success, he did not like that The Rock hadn't returned to wrestling during his pursuit of a film career.

The feud escalated in 2011 when The Rock returned to the WWE. It was announced that the two would square off in a match the following year. Both wrestlers were determined to end that grand match in victory.

Ultimately, it was The Rock who took the match and the title, but Cena stood tall in defeat. His green T-shirt emblazoned with "Rise Above Hate" became a symbol of his spirit and his "Never Give Up" attitude. In fact, he urged his fans to let the bright green color become the symbol for young people all over the world who face bullying.

ONCE FOES, NOW FRIENDS

John Cena confessed that the year the two wrestlers spent "feuding" actually brought them closer.

"We spent a year making fun of each other, and then one night beating each other up," Cena said. After the match they were able to set their differences aside.

Cena even turned to his new friend for some acting advice! "I had an audition . . . and I was really nervous," Cena said. "And I thought, 'Well, I should talk to the one guy who's been in a lot of movies.' And Dwayne just happened to be at WWE [that day]." So he asked Johnson for tips on how to approach the audition, and Johnson gave him a piece of advice "that still rings in my ears," Cena said. "Just be yourself, man," Johnson told him. "That's why they asked you there in the first place."

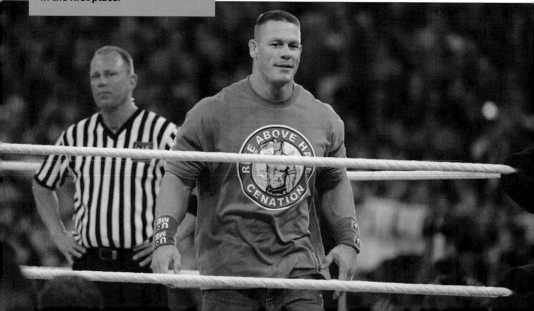

JOHN CENA   VS.   THE ROCK

John Cena	The Rock
Started as a heel (*the bad guy or villain in a pro wrestling storyline.*)	**Started as a heel**
Movie star	**Movie star**
Still with the WWE	**Retired from the WWE**
Rapper: *You Can't See Me*	**Singer:** "You're Welcome" (*Moana*)
Signature move: Five-knuckle shuffle	**Signature move:** People's elbow
Catchphrase: "You Can't See Me"	**Catchphrase:** "If you smell what The Rock is cooking"
Superior mic skills	**Superior mic skills**
Hosted the Kids' Choice Awards (twice)	**Has won 3 Teen Choice Awards**
Voice of Yoshi in *Dolittle*; Baron Draxum in *Rise of the Teenage Mutant Ninja Turtles*	**Voice of** Maui in *Moana*; Captain Charles T. Baker in *Planet 51*
TV host: *American Grit*; *Are You Smarter Than a 5th Grader?*	**TV host:** *The Hero*; *Wake-Up Call*; *The Titan Games*
Legacy Award, 2018	**Image Award,** 2017

FROM RING
TO SCREEN

John Cena has quickly become one of Hollywood's rising stars. Along with his duties hosting Nickelodeon's *Are You Smarter Than a 5th Grader?*, making television appearances, starring in blockbuster films, and doing voiceover work for animated films, John Cena is the busiest pro wrestler . . . who isn't wrestling! While focusing on his acting career, Cena's been spending less time in the ring and more time in front of the camera.

Ferdinand

One of Cena's favorite film projects was lending his very recognizable voice to Ferdinand the bull in animated film *Ferdinand*, based on the popular children's book classic. "I have been living the story of Ferdinand my entire life," Cena says. "He is big and clumsy and vulnerable. He's not afraid to laugh at himself."

Playing with Fire

In 2019, John Cena starred in the comedy film *Playing with Fire* as a no-nonsense smoke jumper. A smoke jumper is a firefighter trained to parachute into remote areas and attack wildfires.

During filming, Cena worked with real smoke jumpers hired as consultants. This experience left a lasting impression on him. Around the release of the film, California was experiencing devastating wildfires. In honor of the film and National First Responders Day (October 28, 2019), Cena pledged to donate half a million dollars to an organization chosen by Paramount, the studio that made the film. Paramount matched Cena's donation and chose the Los Angeles Fire Department Foundation and California Fire Foundation to receive the total $1 million donation.

"What sets first responders apart," Cena says, "is that an ordinary day of work can include willingly facing down danger. I admire that because it is something I have trouble doing. I enjoy doing stunts, but when something doesn't seem too safe, I'm like, 'We should talk this over . . .'"

Dolittle

John Cena was also part of the movie *Dolittle*. Cena voiced Yoshi, the funny, upbeat polar bear. The wrestler-turned-actor says what made Yoshi's scenes so great was the fact that he shared most of them with Kumail Nanjiani, the actor who voiced Plimpton, the cynical ostrich.

TV Host with the Most

Cena credits the WWE for helping to prepare him for his hosting duties on Nickelodeon's *Are You Smarter Than a 5th Grader*?

"We have the same goals," Cena says of Nickelodeon and the WWE. "We want to put smiles on people's faces. That literally is Nickelodeon's ethos and it is one that the WWE shares and one that I certainly agree with. When you want to make kids and families happy, it makes it a lot easier."

Every episode has Cena going for big laughs. Whether he's dancing in a ballerina's tutu, playing his WWE entrance song on the recorder (badly!), or learning how to "pageant walk" from one of the kids on the show, his goal is to make sure everybody is having fun!

American Grit

Thanks to his many travels visiting US soldiers in Afghanistan, Iraq, and Army bases in the United States with WWE's annual Tribute to the Troops event, John Cena has developed a deep connection to the men and women of America's armed forces. In 2016 and 2017, he hosted a reality TV show called *American Grit*, featuring veterans who helped other veterans stay in shape after their tours. Most recently, John worked with FitOps, an organization that helps veterans rejoin civilian society by becoming personal trainers.

The wrestling superstar has become so passionate about FitOps and its mission that in 2019 he announced he would personally match every donation the organization received, up to $1 million.

Talking Trash Bags

Everyone knows you don't mess with John Cena.

But guess what? You don't mess with his mom either!

Just a few years ago, John Cena fans were thrilled to see the wrestling icon starring in funny TV commercials for trash bags . . . with his mother. In the over-the-top spots, Carol Cena puts her son in a near-perfect headlock when he's about to buy cheaper, flimsier trash bags! The move sent Cenation fans into gales of laughter, making the commercial one of the most popular ads of the year.

"I couldn't have asked for a better co-star than my mom," Cena said in an interview. "She has an amazing sense of humor and is the epitome of a strong woman, having raised five boys."

CENA'S NEXT MOVE

Looking back, Cena says his entire career—

the wrestling, the acting, his enthusiastic support for good causes—
was all impossible to imagine when he was a small-town kid growing
up in northeast Massachusetts. And even years later, he still had his
doubts he would become a successful wrestler. "This is out of my
league," he thought when he saw the other bigger, stronger wrestlers.

Still, he figured he had nothing to lose by trying. "I'm just gonna
go for it," Cena told himself back then. And that's the way he has
operated ever since that time. "It's let me take chances that a lot of the
other superstars are afraid to take," he says.

Decades later, now that he's achieved his dreams and beyond, John
Cena is the first to admit that the physical demands of pro wrestling
are taking a toll on his body. He gets asked all the time if he's thinking
of quitting wrestling for good. "As long as they find me entertaining,"
he replies every time, "I will do my best to go out there and entertain!"

He isn't worrying about what comes next, either. As he continues
his acting career and starring in upcoming blockbusters, he also
hasn't ruled out trying for another championship title. But the most
important part, he says, is focusing on what makes him happy and
gives his life meaning. At the moment, that includes doing a little bit
of everything: acting, writing, hosting game shows, voicing animations,
and making wrestling appearances!

"I love what I do," Cena
says. "I just know that
it's going to end at some
point, so I kind of want
to enjoy it all!"

"We all have to earn
a living, but if you can
also affect people?
That's a good deal.
It gives me the feeling
like, yeah, I'm in the
right place and I'm
doing the right thing
with my life."

—JOHN CENA